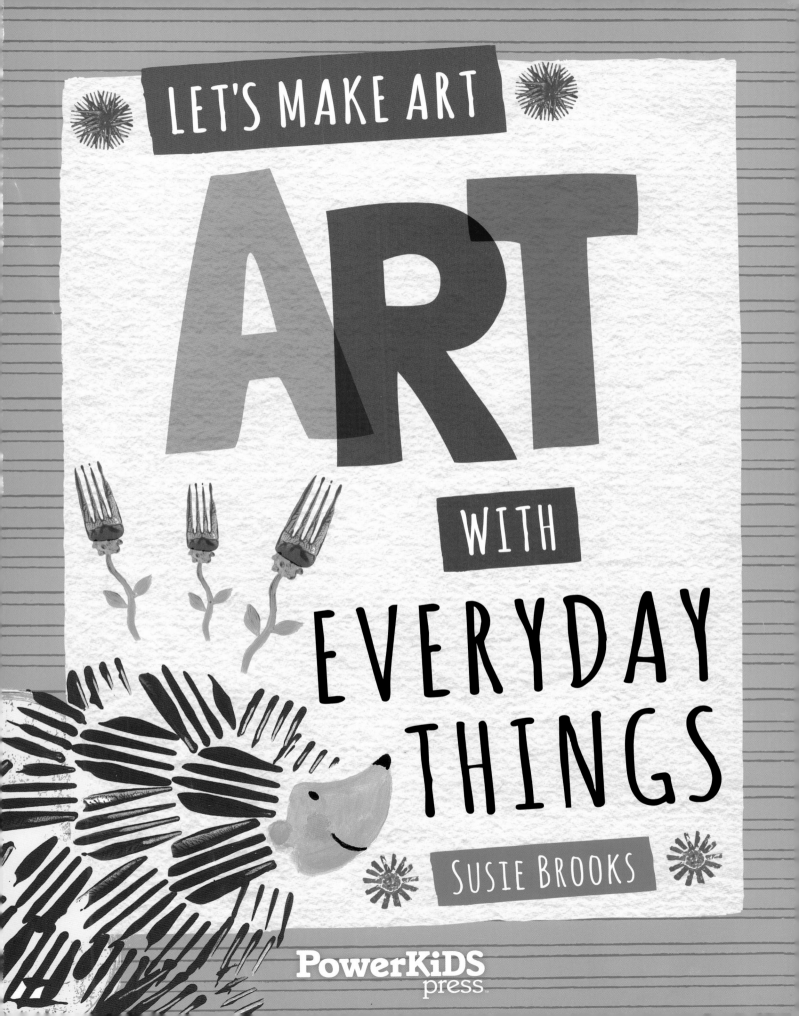

LET'S MAKE ART

ART

WITH

EVERYDAY THINGS

Susie Brooks

PowerKiDS press

Published in 2018 by **The Rosen Publishing Group, Inc.**
29 East 21st Street, New York, NY 10010

Cataloging-in-Publication Data
Names: Brooks, Susie.
Title: Art with everyday things / Susie Brooks.
Description: New York : PowerKids Press, 2018. | Series: Let's make art | Includes index.
Identifiers: ISBN 9781538323144 (pbk.) | ISBN 9781538322192 (library bound) |
   ISBN 9781538323151 (6 pack)
Subjects: LCSH: Handicraft--Juvenile literature.
Classification: LCC TT160.B76 2018 | DDC 745.5--dc23

Editor: Elizabeth Brent
Design: nicandlou

Manufactured in China
CPSIA Compliance Information: Batch BW18PK: For Further Information contact
Rosen Publishing, New York, New York at 1-800-237-9932.

CONTENTS

LET'S MAKE ART!

Look all around you, indoors and outdoors — what can you find to make into art? This book is packed with exciting ideas to help you turn ordinary things into extraordinary works of art!

WHAT YOU NEED

Search at home for things that you can print with, paint on, cut out, or trace. In this book, we'll make art using coins, keys, paper towels, plastic wrap, toilet rolls, popsicle sticks, sponges, forks, cheese graters, twist ties, and even salt and soap! Check your recycling bin for old newspaper, envelopes, and cereal boxes and save them for your work too.

FOR THE PROJECTS IN THIS BOOK IT ALSO HELPS TO HAVE A FEW BASIC ART SUPPLIES:

✓ A PENCIL AND ERASER
✓ PAINT
✓ PAINTBRUSHES
✓ PAPER PLATES OR A PAINT PALETTE
✓ COLORED INK PADS
✓ MARKERS
✓ CRAYONS OR OIL PASTELS
✓ SCISSORS
✓ GLUE
✓ PLAIN WHITE PAPER OR CARD STOCK
✓ COLORED PAPER OR CARD STOCK, INCLUDING BLACK
✓ STRING, THREAD, OR YARN
✓ A HOLE PUNCH
✓ NEWSPAPER

HANDY HINTS

Before you start, lay down plenty of newspaper to protect the surface you're working on.

Painted paper will dry more quickly if you leave it in a warm place, such as by a sunny window or by a radiator.

Sometimes painted paper wrinkles as it dries. Don't worry — you can flatten it later under a pile of books.

Always wait for your paint to dry before drawing or gluing on details.

If you don't have paper in the color you want, you can always paint your own.

Nail clippers are handy for cutting small paper shapes. Some craft scissors have a special zigzag blade for fancy edges.

There are templates on pages 30-31 to help you draw some useful shapes, but don't try to copy everything exactly. Half the fun of art is using your imagination and testing ideas of your own!

When you see this logo, you might want to ask an adult to help.

FANTASIC FORKS

PRINT THESE FUN ANIMALS WITH AN EVERYDAY FORK — BUT REMEMBER TO WASH THE PAINT OFF AFTERWARDS!

1 Spread some paint onto a paper plate and dip in the back of a fork. Practice making prong prints, like below, onto white paper.

2 To make a cat, print a round head like this. For the body, make several rows of prints underneath each other.

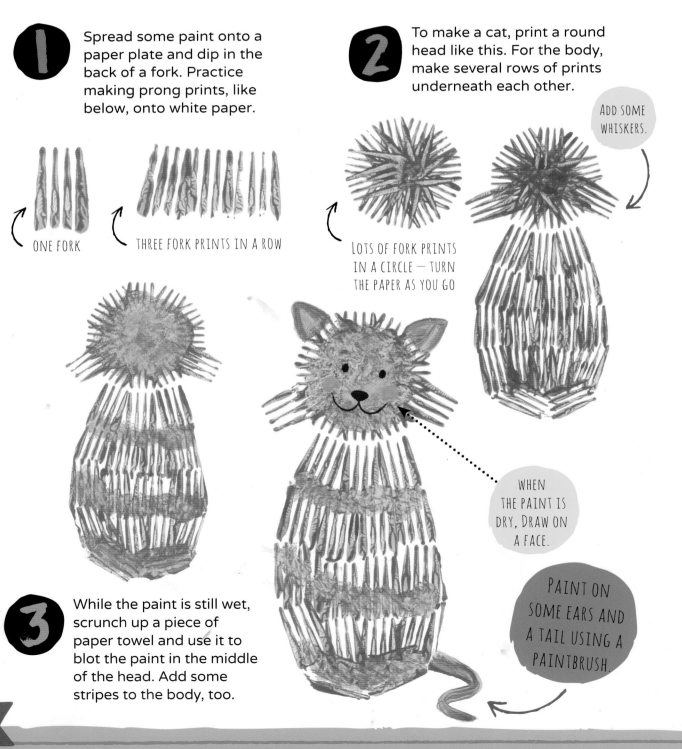

ONE FORK

THREE FORK PRINTS IN A ROW

LOTS OF FORK PRINTS IN A CIRCLE — TURN THE PAPER AS YOU GO

ADD SOME WHISKERS.

WHEN THE PAINT IS DRY, DRAW ON A FACE.

PAINT ON SOME EARS AND A TAIL USING A PAINTBRUSH.

3 While the paint is still wet, scrunch up a piece of paper towel and use it to blot the paint in the middle of the head. Add some stripes to the body, too.

WHAT OTHER ANIMALS
CAN YOU PRINT?

TRY A WHITE SHEEP...

OR A HEDGEHOG...

USE COLORED PAPER. WHY NOT FORK-PRINT SOME GREEN GRASS?

OR "FORKUPINE"! PRINT THE FORKY SPINES FIRST, THEN PAINT ON A HEAD.

OR SOME FORK FLOWERS!

PRESS THE FORK DOWN AND ROCK IT BACKWARDS TO PRINT THE PART BELOW THE PRONGS. THEN PAINT ON A STALK AND LEAVES, AND YOU HAVE A FLOWER!

BEAUTIFUL BALLOONS

USE SCRAPS OF OLD FABRIC, FELT, OR PAPER TOWEL TO MAKE THIS HOT-AIR BALLOON COLLAGE!

1 Start by making a balloon template. Fold a piece of paper in half. Draw a shape like this by the folded edge.

CUT OUT THE SHAPE AND OPEN IT OUT LIKE THIS TO MAKE A TEMPLATE.

2 Cut several strips of fabric, a bit longer than the template's width. Glue them in stripes onto another piece of paper until you have a block that's as tall as the template.

3 Trace your template on the fabric block and cut out the balloon shape. Glue it onto a piece of white paper.

4 Now make the basket. Cut a shape from fabric and glue it about 1 inch (2 cm) below the balloon. Glue two pieces of thread or wool between the two.

FINGERPRINT A PERSON TO GO IN THE BASKET.

WHY NOT MAKE A COLLECTION OF BALLOONS?

Cut square pieces of fabric and arrange them in a block. Glue them on to paper before cutting out the balloon, as you did in Step 2.

You can cut fancy edges with zigzag craft scissors.

Add a face, hair, and some waving arms to your person!

TIP

Thumbprint some birds, then draw on beaks, wings, and tails. You could stick fabric clouds above them and draw lines to make them look as if they're dangling!

This bush was cut from an old sock.

ICE CREAM BUNTING

RECYCLE CARDBOARD INTO A DELICIOUS DECORATION!
OLD CEREAL BOXES WORK WELL FOR THIS PROJECT.

1 Draw a diamond shape on a piece of white cardboard, as shown. If your cardboard is not white, glue some white paper over it. You'll need at least five or six of these shapes.

THERE ARE TEMPLATES FOR SOME OF THE SHAPES ON P. 30.

2 Cut out the shapes and use a hole punch to make two holes in the top part, like this.

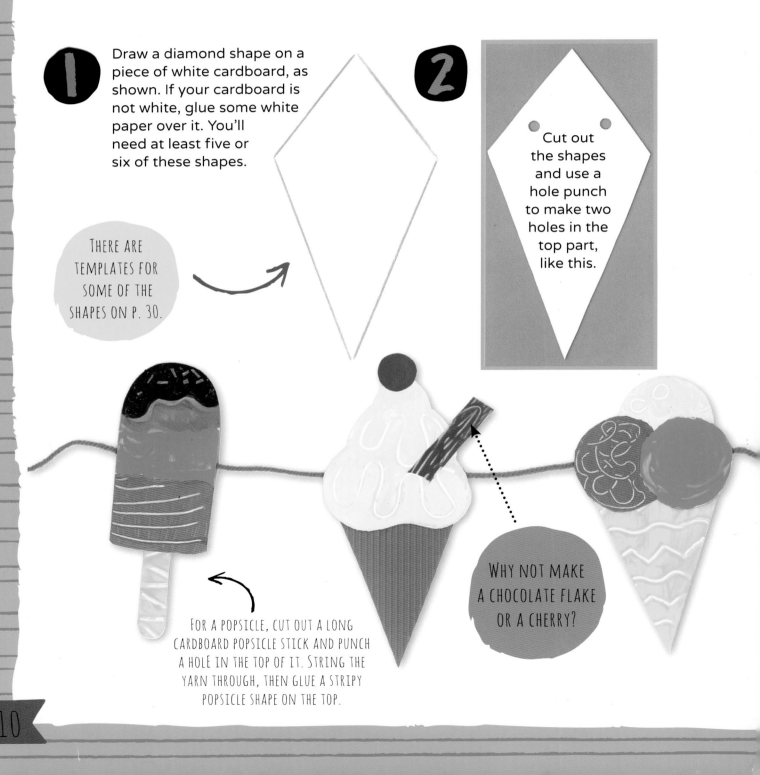

FOR A POPSICLE, CUT OUT A LONG CARDBOARD POPSICLE STICK AND PUNCH A HOLE IN THE TOP OF IT. STRING THE YARN THROUGH, THEN GLUE A STRIPY POPSICLE SHAPE ON THE TOP.

WHY NOT MAKE A CHOCOLATE FLAKE OR A CHERRY?

Mix some yellow paint with a little flour or white glue to thicken it. Use this to paint the cones. While the paint is wet, scratch patterns into it using the end of your brush.

4 Cut out some ice cream shapes from white cardboard — one for each cone. Paint them with thickened paint, as in Step 3. Swirl patterns into the paint. You could use glitter or even real sugar sprinkles to decorate!

TIP

The paint will take several hours to dry. Be patient! You could try another project while you wait.

 When the paint is dry, string your cones onto a long piece of thread. Space them out and glue an ice cream shape over each cone.

YOUR BUNTING IS READY TO HANG!

Try using nail polish for a drizzle of sauce.

COOL CROCODILES

PAINT PAPER TOWELS TO MAKE THIS SUPER-SCALY CROCODILE COLLAGE!

1 Lay a sheet of paper towel on some newspaper. Use thin, watery paint to color the paper towel green and yellow. Leave it to dry.

THE COLORS WILL RUN INTO EACH OTHER!

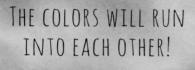

2 When the paper is dry, cut out or tear shapes like these for a crocodile.

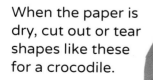

3 Glue the shapes onto a piece of white paper. Paint on two white eyes with black dots in the middle. You could tear some small strips from the leftover green paper towel and glue them to the tail to make stripes.

Try painting more paper towels in different colors. When they're dry, tear strips of blue for a lake, and glue them near your crocodile's feet.

Add some paper claws if you like.

Why not add a swimming croc in the lake?

You could cut out and stick on some birds, reeds, and lilies. There are some templates on p. 31 if you need them.

SOAPY SOLAR SYSTEM

MIX WATERY PAINT WITH SOAP AND SALT TO MAKE A PICTURE THAT'S OUT OF THIS WORLD!

 Rub a bar of soap back and forth over a piece of white card stock or paper. Brush watery paint over the top and leave it to dry. You'll get a streaky effect like this.

 When the paint is dry, trace around a cup and cut out circles for planets.

Cut a strip like this and glue it across a planet for a ring.

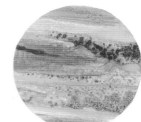

 For a speckled effect, sprinkle salt over the wet paint and brush it off when dry.

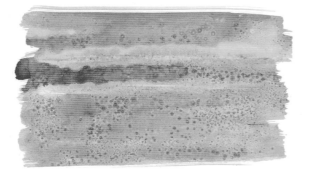

YOU COULD USE ZIGZAG CRAFT SCISSORS TO MAKE A FIERY SUN OR STARS.

TIP
WHILE THE PAINT IS DRYING, REPEAT Step 1 IN A FEW DIFFERENT COLORS AND PAINT THE BACKGROUND FOR Step 4.

4 For your spacey background, swirl the bar of soap in a spiral over a large sheet of white card stock or paper. Brush watery, dark-blue paint all over it and let it dry.

GLUE ON YOUR PLANETS, STARS, AND SUN. YOU COULD ADD AN ALIEN OR A SHOOTING STAR!

KEY CARTOONS

USE KEYS TO MAKE THESE PRINTS, THEN TURN THEM INTO QUIRKY CARTOON CHARACTERS.

1 Ask an adult for a spare key that you can use. Press it on to a colored ink pad, then print it on white paper.

3 Try making two key prints with the narrow ends together.

2 For a dog, draw a circle with a loop on top, like this.

THEY COULD BECOME A FACE...

...OR AN OWL!

SCRIBBLE THE EARS AND NECK, AND DRAW IN EYES AND A SMILEY MOUTH.

THERE ARE TEMPLATES ON P. 30 IF YOU NEED THEM.

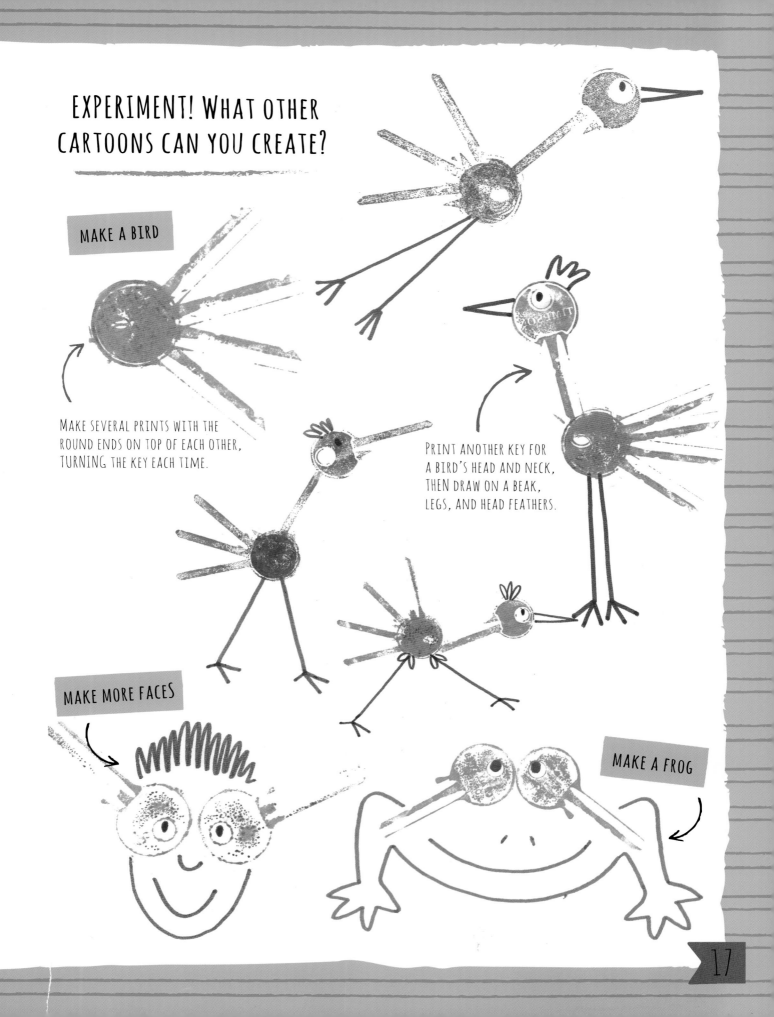

EXPERIMENT! WHAT OTHER CARTOONS CAN YOU CREATE?

MAKE A BIRD

MAKE SEVERAL PRINTS WITH THE ROUND ENDS ON TOP OF EACH OTHER, TURNING THE KEY EACH TIME.

PRINT ANOTHER KEY FOR A BIRD'S HEAD AND NECK, THEN DRAW ON A BEAK, LEGS, AND HEAD FEATHERS.

MAKE MORE FACES

MAKE A FROG

TEXTURED TURTLES

MAKE AN UNDERWATER WORLD BY PRINTING WITH PLASTIC WRAP!

1 Tear off a piece of plastic wrap at least the size of a sheet of paper. Lay it over newspaper, and then use a damp sponge to cover it with blue paint. Press a piece of white paper on top, then peel the paper off.

2 While the paper is drying, make a couple more plastic wrap prints using yellow and green paper. When they are dry, cut out shapes for a turtle (there are templates on p. 31).

TIP

TRY A FEW PRINTS — YOU'LL GET DIFFERENT TEXTURES DEPENDING ON HOW WATERY YOUR PAINT IS.

3 Glue the turtle onto the blue background. You could cut out some oval shapes in a different color and stick them on the shell, too.

MAKE PLASTIC WRAP PRINTS ON DIFFERENT COLORS OF PAPER TO MAKE ROCKS AND STARFISH!

MONEY TREES

USE A CLUSTER OF COINS TO MAKE SOME MAGICAL MONEY TREES!

 Try to use a mixture of different coins. Lay a piece of thin paper over a coin and rub a wax crayon on the surface.

 For a brighter effect, brush watery paint over your rubbing. The crayon will resist the paint! Don't worry about neat edges — you're going to cut the coins out.

TIP
HOLD THE PAPER OVER THE COIN WITH ONE FINGER, TO KEEP IT STEADY AS YOU WORK.

3 Make lots of colorful rubbings and cut them out. Keep them safe while you paint a white tree trunk and branches onto colored paper. You could scratch lines into the trunk using the end of your brush to look like bark. Let it dry.

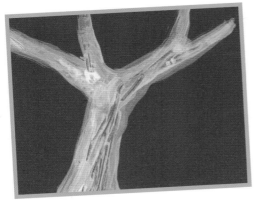

 Now glue your paper coins onto your tree, like leaves.

HERE ARE SOME OTHER IDEAS YOU CAN TRY...

LUCKY BOUQUET

Cut strips of green paper for stalks and glue them down. Glue on a piece of doily, then glue a cluster of coins on top. Add two paper triangles and a square for the bow.

TREE IN A TUB

Glue down a cluster of coins. Glue on a trunk shape cut from colored paper, and a piece of a cupcake wrapper for a pot.

GLUE ALL THE COIN RUBBINGS ONTO COLORED PAPER.

CHRISTMAS TREE

Cut out a green paper triangle and a yellow trunk. Glue on pieces of doily for decoration and stick the coins on top.

YOU COULD FOLD THE PAPER FIRST, TO MAKE A GREETING CARD WITH A LUCKY COIN TREE ON THE FRONT.

SPONGY SNOWMEN

USE A SPONGE AND A CARDBOARD STENCIL TO PAINT A FLURRY OF SNOWMAN FRIENDS.

 To make the stencil, draw two circles like this onto thin cardboard. You can use cups or rolls of tape as a guide. Cut out the shape, keeping the outside piece whole.

 Now lay the stencil on a larger piece of cardboard. Dip a sponge in thick white paint and dab it all over the cut-out shape.

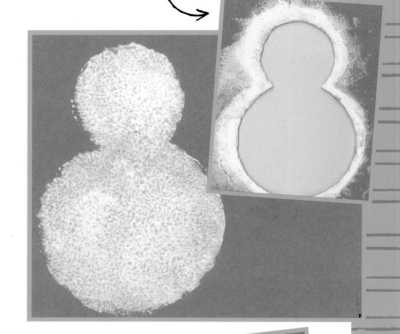

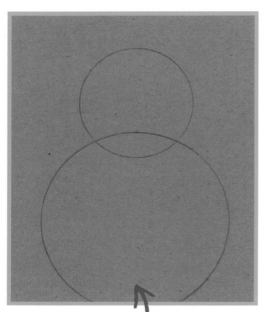

TIP
If you keep the inside piece too, you can use it for the puppet on p. 24!

3 Use the sponge to paint a line of snow at the bottom. Tear off a small piece of sponge to paint some snowflakes.

4 Cut a strip of sponge and cover one edge in black paint. Press it down to print two arms. Print the eyes and buttons with the end of a pencil, and paint a line of dots for the mouth.

5 Now dress up your snowman! Use your sponge to dab colored paint on to paper.

TRY A CLOWN HAT, BOW TIE OR SOME SUNGLASSES!

CUT OUT HAT AND SCARF SHAPES TO STICK ON.

HAT

SCARF

CUT OUT A TRIANGULAR NOSE FROM ORANGE CARDBOARD AND STICK IT ON.

POPSICLE STICK PUPPETS

THESE PUPPETS ARE A GREAT WAY TO RECYCLE OLD FOOD PACKAGING AND POPSICLE STICKS.

 Draw two circles like this on a piece of thin cardboard, as you did for the snowman on p. 22. Cut out the whole shape.

 Cut a circle of white paper, the same size as the big circle, and paint or glue on red stripes. Glue this onto your cardboard shape.

THERE ARE TEMPLATES ON P. 31 IF YOU NEED THEM.

 Paint or glue on a beard shape. This one was cut from a magazine. Draw on a face with an eyepatch.

4 Cut out a black pirate's hat and paint on white crossbones. Cut out a cardboard hand, hook, and boot. Glue each one to a wire twist tie or pipe cleaner and tape them in place at the back of the pirate's body.

HOOK

HAND

PIRATE HAT

BOOT

5 Tape the other end of each arm and leg to the back of the pirate's body. Glue the hat onto the head. You could stick on a sword cut from tinfoil.

WHAT OTHER PUPPET CHARACTERS CAN YOU MAKE?

TAPE ON A POPSICLE STICK FOR A HANDLE THAT DOUBLES AS A WOODEN LEG!

TRY AN ASTRONAUT

STICK TWO CIRCLES OF NEWSPAPER ONTO ANOTHER CARDBOARD BASE AS BEFORE. DECORATE WITH SHAPES CUT FROM COLORED PAPER AND TINFOIL.

MAKE A THUMBPRINT ON A SMALL CIRCLE OF WHITE PAPER. DRAW ON A FACE AND GLUE IT ON THE ASTRONAUT'S HEAD.

FLOWERS AND FIREWORKS

CREATE SOME BRIGHT DESIGNS WITH A TOILET PAPER ROLL!

1. Start by cutting slits up from one end of the tube. The slits should be about 2 inches (5 cm) long and roughly 0.5 inches (1 cm) apart.

SPLAY OUT THE SPLIT ENDS, LIKE THIS.

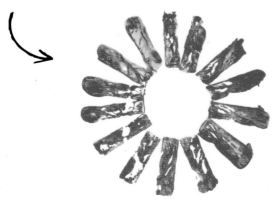

2. Squeeze some red and yellow paint onto a paper plate. Dip the splayed end of the tube into it and move it around until the strips are all coated. Press the tube onto paper, and you'll get a shape like this.

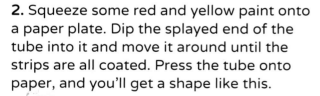

3. You could turn your pattern into a flower or a sun. Use your fingertip to print dots in the middle. Paint in a stalk and leaves, or cut them from green paper and glue them on.

PROJECT 2

For a firework display, add some white paint to your plate and print on black paper. Dip the splayed ends of the tube back into the paint for each firework.

SPONGE SOME RED AND YELLOW PAINT OVER THEM SO THEY GLOW!

YOU COULD CUT OUT SOME BUILDING SHAPES FROM NEWSPAPER AND GLUE THEM BELOW THE FIREWORKS.

PATCHWORK PATTERNS

YOU CAN MAKE CRAYON RUBBINGS FROM ALL SORTS OF EVERYDAY ITEMS AND TURN THEM INTO BEAUTIFUL DESIGNS.

1 Find a few things that have an interesting texture on their surface. The examples on this page will give you some ideas. Lay a piece of thin paper over each one and rub with a crayon or oil pastel.

THESE PATTERNS CAME FROM THE DIFFERENT SIDES OF A CHEESE GRATER.

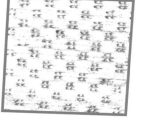

FOR STRIPES TRY:

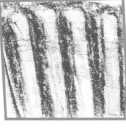

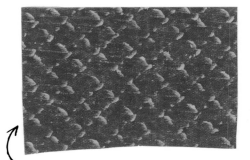

CORRUGATED CARDBOARD

A GRIDDLE PAN

A SLOTTED SPATULA

TRY RUBBING GENTLY ON COLORED TISSUE PAPER

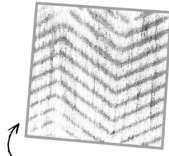

A MESH BAG

THE BOTTOM OF A SHOE

PATTERNS ON CARVED FURNITURE, BELT BUCKLES, OR TRINKETS

2 Make a selection of rubbings, then cut out squares, rectangles, circles, and triangles from them. Arrange them in patterns and glue them onto scrap paper.

TRY MAKING A POSTCARD!

CUT STRIPS OF A SIMILAR WIDTH AND ARRANGE THEM AROUND A PICTURE, LIKE A FRAME!

SMALLER SHAPES MAKE GREAT GIFT TAGS OR BOOKMARKS.

YOU COULD TAPE A TOOTHPICK TO THE BACK FOR A FUN FLAG DECORATION.

29

TEMPLATES

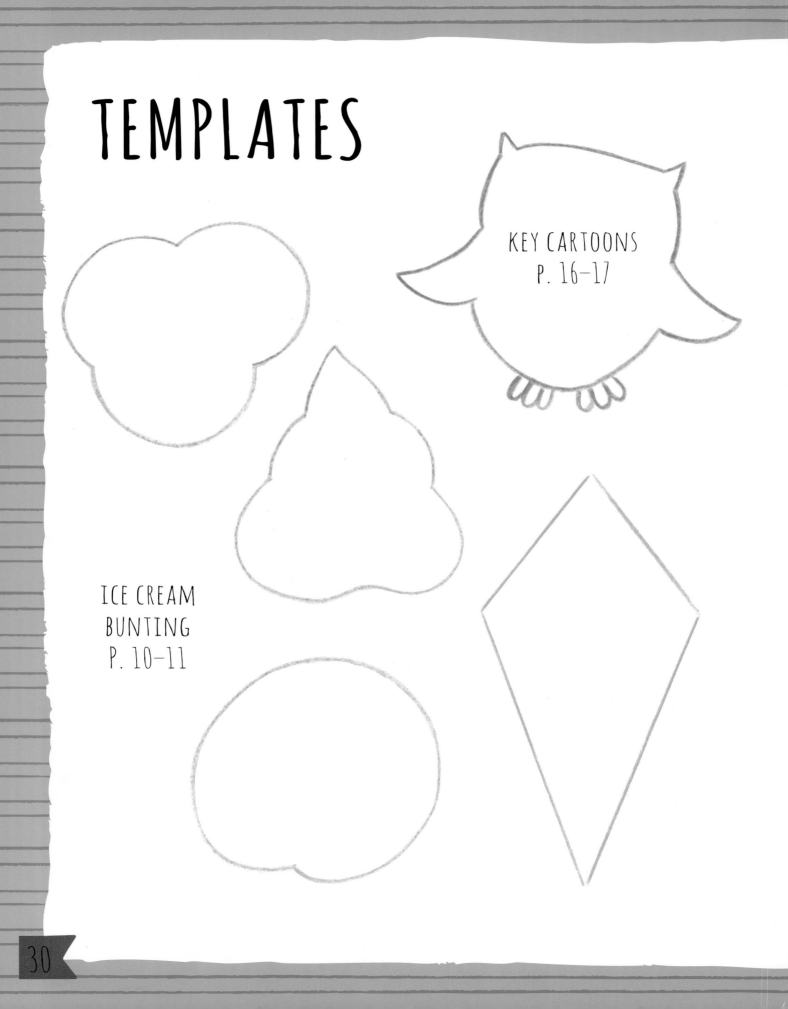

KEY CARTOONS
P. 16–17

ICE CREAM
BUNTING
P. 10–11

TEXTURED TURTLES
P. 18–19

Popsicle Stick
Puppets
P. 24–25

Cool Crocodiles
P. 12–13

GLOSSARY

COLLAGE: ART MADE BY GLUING PIECES OF PAPER, FABRIC, OR OTHER MATERIALS ON TO A SURFACE

CORRUGATED: RIDGED, LIKE THE INSIDE LAYER OF SOME CARDBOARD

PRINT: TO MAKE AN IMAGE BY PRESSING A PAINTED OR INKED OBJECT ONTO PAPER, OR ANOTHER SURFACE

SPLAYED: SPREAD OUT AND APART

STENCIL: A THIN PIECE OF CARDBOARD (OR OTHER MATERIAL) WITH A SHAPE CUT OUT OF IT

TEMPLATE: A SHAPE USED AS A GUIDELINE TO TRACE

TEXTURE: THE FEEL OR APPEARANCE OF A SURFACE, SUCH AS FLUFFY WOOL